To Paige—you are a force of nature

Copyright © 2019 by Lily Williams
Published by Roaring Brook Press
Roaring Brook Press is a division of Holtzbrinck Publishing Holdings Limited Partnership
120 Broadway, New York, NY 10271

mackids.com

Library of Congress Control Number: 2019932710
ISBN 978-1-250-14320-4

Our books may be purchased in bulk for promotional, educational, or business use.
Please contact your local bookseller or the Macmillan Corporate and Premium Sales Department
at (800) 221-7945 ext. 5442 or by email at MacmillanSpecialMarkets@macmillan.com.

First edition, 2019
Printed in China by Toppan Leefung Printing Ltd., Dongguan City, Guangdong Province

10 9 8 7 6 5 4 3 2 1

IF ELEPHANTS DISAPPEARED

Lily Williams

ROARING BROOK PRESS
NEW YORK

THIS IS THE CONGO BASIN FOREST. It's a
complex ecosystem filled with many different
types of landscapes, plants, and animals. The
animals that live here are
        strong,
            slippery,
                loud, and . . .

BIG.

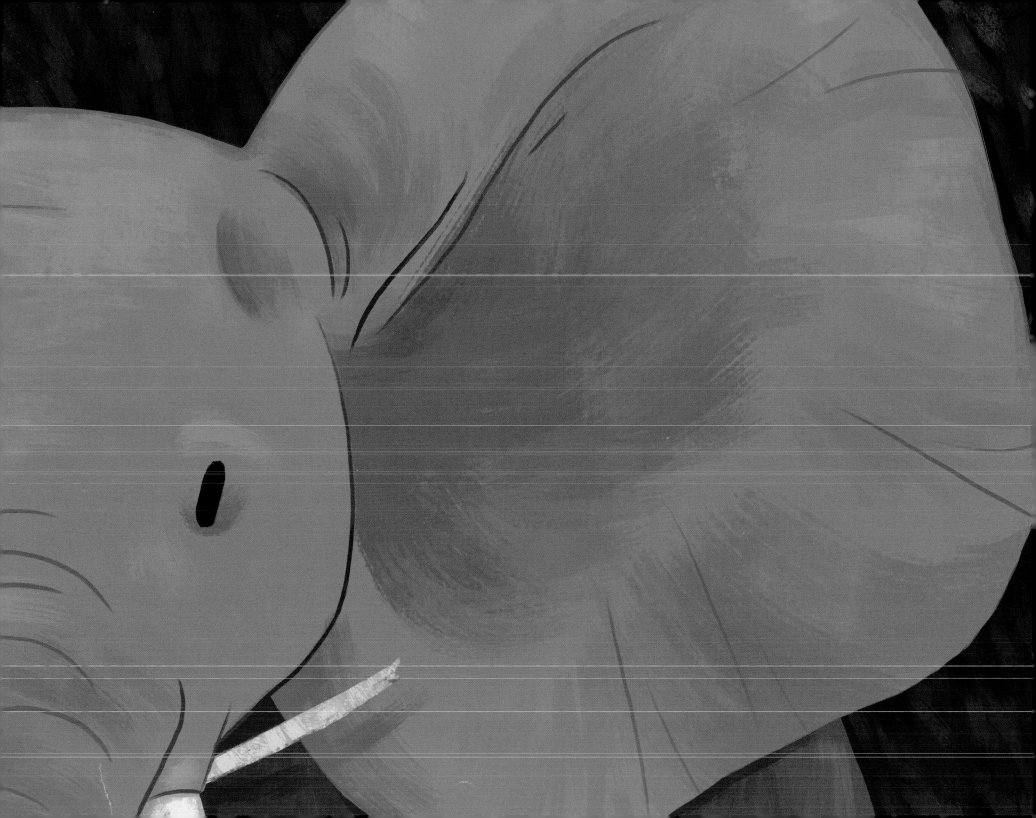

BIG BANG
13.8 BILLION YEARS AGO

FORMATION OF EARTH ABOUT 4.6 BILLION YEARS AGO

FIRST LIFE ON EARTH 3-3.5 BILLION YEARS AGO

530 MILLION YEARS AGO

LIFE ON EARTH BECOMES MORE COMPLEX

TALL TREES MADE FORESTS

250 MILLION YEARS AGO

BIG EXTINCTION

FIRST REPTILES AND MODERN PLANTS APPEARED

MASS EXTINCTION
60-65 MILLION YEARS AGO

FIRST ELEPHANT ANCESTORS APPEARED

ELEPHANT SPECIES DIVERGED 1.9-6.7 MILLION YEARS AGO

AFRICAN FOREST ELEPHANT

Elephants' first ancestors arose in Africa about 60 million years ago and eventually split into the three playful species that we know today—the African forest elephant, African savanna elephant, and Asian elephant. The African forest elephant is the smaller of the African species, growing to around ten feet tall and weighing over 11,000 pounds. Still, it's one of the largest land mammals on Earth.

450 MILLION YEARS AGO
FIRST SHARKS APPEARED

HUMANS APPEARED
200,000 YEARS AGO

TODAY!

AFRICAN SAVANNA ELEPHANT

Elephants are a keystone species, which means that their actions—from walking, to eating, to pooping, to sleeping—shape their environment. Without keystone species, the ecosystems they live in, such as African

In order to feed their big bodies, elephants will walk for miles and miles each day consuming several hundred pounds of fruits, branches, bark, roots, grasses, and leaves. All that eating and walking spreads their poop far and wide.

Because elephants have inefficient digestive systems, their poop, called dung, is full of thousands of undigested seeds that increase the forests' plant biodiversity by moving the seeds from one place to another.

Today, elephants are hunted for their ivory tusks, which are displayed whole or carved into trinkets. Poachers are killing elephants faster than the elephants can reproduce. Roughly 62 percent of African forest elephants were lost between 2001 and 2018.

2001

THE AFRICAN FOREST
ELEPHANT POPULATION
DECLINED BY ROUGHLY
62% FROM 2001 TO
2018

LIVING ELEPHANT   DECEASED ELEPHANT

If elephants disappeared . . .

2018

so would their dung, which is filled with thousands of seeds from the many different plants that the elephants eat. When elephants eat plants with seeds, the seeds soften and sprout from the acid in their digestive systems. When those seeds are passed, the nutrient-rich dung surrounding them fertilizes and protects them so they grow faster than seeds planted in the ground. Some plants have evolved to make elephant dung the only way their seeds can be spread.

If elephant dung disappeared . . .

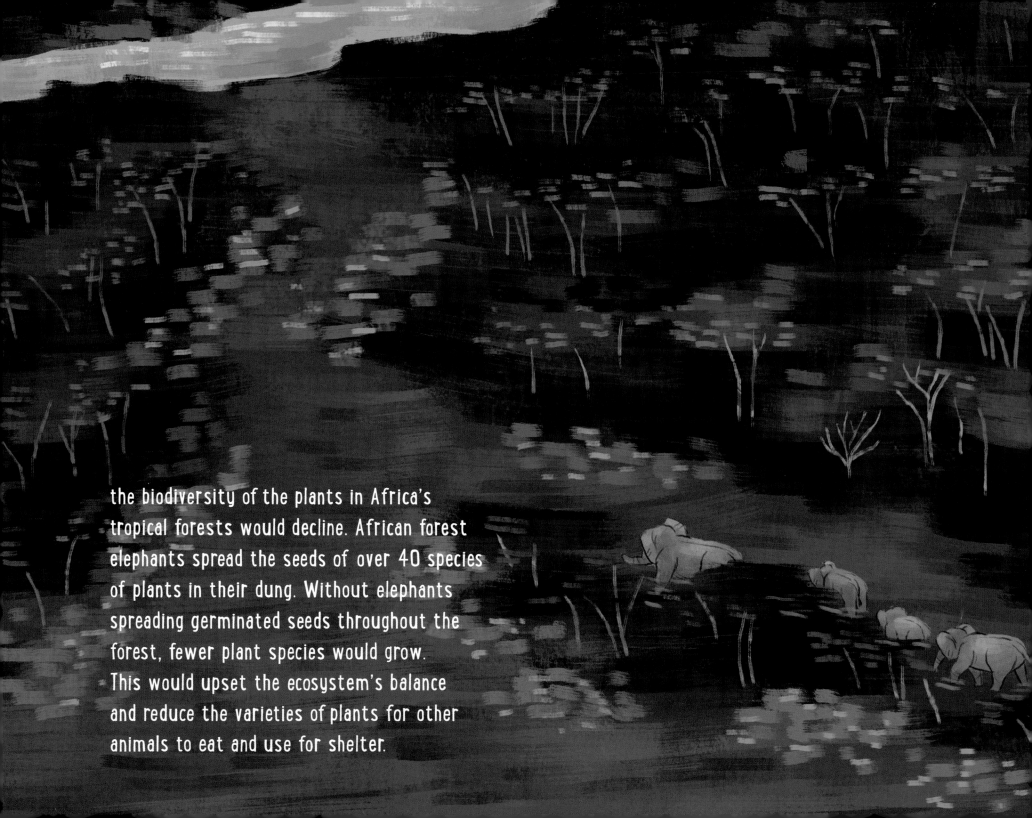

the biodiversity of the plants in Africa's tropical forests would decline. African forest elephants spread the seeds of over 40 species of plants in their dung. Without elephants spreading germinated seeds throughout the forest, fewer plant species would grow. This would upset the ecosystem's balance and reduce the varieties of plants for other animals to eat and use for shelter.

If plant biodiversity disappeared . . .

the large trees would take over the forest. Though large trees reduce harmful greenhouse gases in the atmosphere by capturing carbon in the air and storing it, they also depend on fast-growing smaller plants to create biodiversity in the forest. Larger trees would dominate the forest, crowding out space

for themselves and other species. The change in plant life would affect the forest soil, causing erosion, floods, and even differences in the amount of rainfall the area gets.

If too many plant species disappeared . . .

the forest might not be able to survive. Forests are
complex ecosystems that rely on many different plants
and animals to stay healthy.

Without diverse plant life to provide multiple
kinds of food and shelter, the animals that once
survived in the forest would starve and die out.

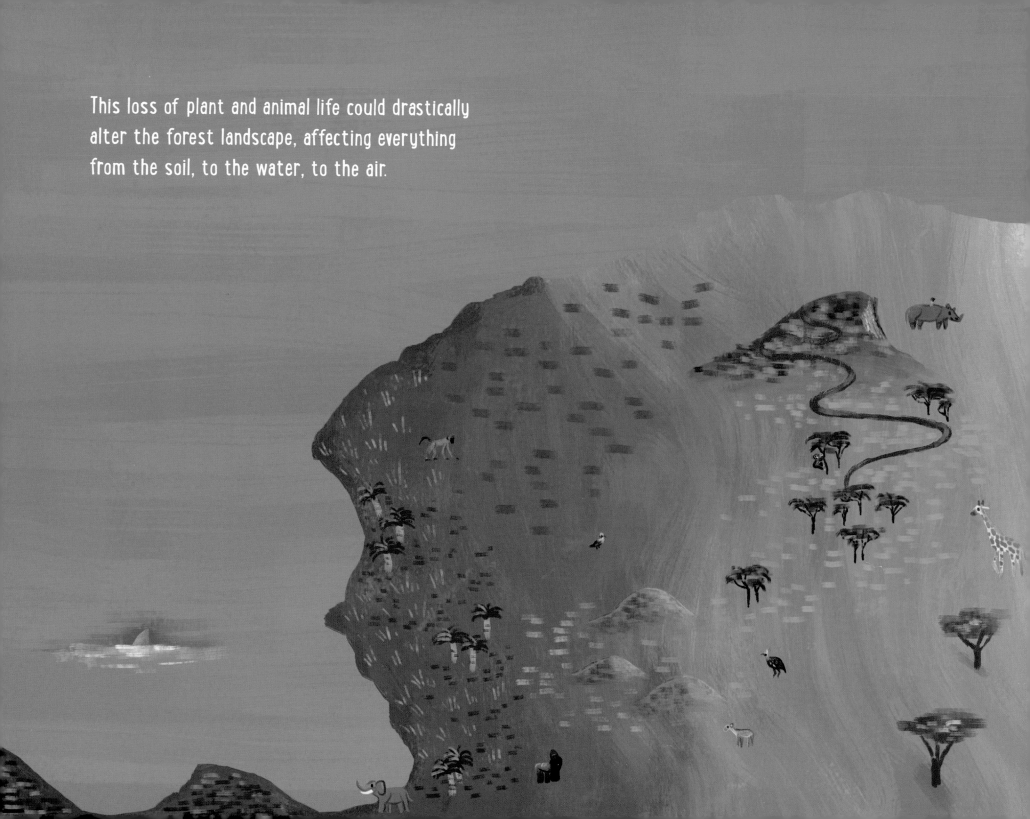

This loss of plant and animal life could drastically alter the forest landscape, affecting everything from the soil, to the water, to the air.

This chain effect, called a trophic cascade,
would spread across different ecosystems,
eventually changing . . .

the world as we know it.

From dung, to plants, to animals, to people, all life on Earth is intricately connected and balanced, and each organism plays a part in helping the world to thrive.

And luckily, today . . .

elephants still roam free. To help, we can use our voices to speak up for those who cannot speak for themselves. And maybe then everyone will see that even the biggest of us . . .

needs a little help now and again.

biodiversity
congo
forests

African forest elephants

GLOSSARY

BIODIVERSITY: the variety of living organisms in a specific area.

CONGO BASIN FOREST: a tropical rain forest in central Africa that is home to swamps and is very hot and humid.

DUNG: an animal's poop.

ECOSYSTEM: a system of living and nonliving things interacting in an environment.

ENVIRONMENT: all the living and nonliving things in a place or region.

EXTINCTION: the deaths, or inability to reproduce, of the last individuals of a species.

GERMINATE: the process where a new plant sprouts out of a seed.

GREENHOUSE GAS: a gas, such as carbon dioxide and methane, that absorbs infrared radiation from the Sun, trapping heat and creating a "greenhouse effect" of warming temperatures on Earth.

HERBIVORE: an animal that eats only plants.

KEYSTONE SPECIES: a species that shapes its ecosystem so much that the ecosystem would be far different without that species.

ORGANISM: a life form (a plant, animal, or single-celled entity).

POACHER: a person who hunts illegally on land where hunting is not allowed, often targeting endangered species.

ALL ELEPHANTS ARE IN TROUBLE

All three species of African and Asian elephants are in trouble. In the early 1900s, there were an estimated 12 million elephants in Africa. In 1970, there were 3 million, and in 2013, an estimated 410,000 to 650,000 African elephants were left. Asian elephants are also endangered, with their populations having gone from 1 million in 1900 to today, when an estimated 38,534 to 52,566 wild elephants remain. The main cause of these declines is the ivory trade, which has slowed since an international ban on buying and selling ivory took effect in 1990, but the illegal trade that occurs worldwide still drives poaching. Historically, elephants' ivory tusks have been used to make everything from dominos to the tops of piano keys, in addition to works of art either carved or used whole as decorative statues.

Elephants are also threatened by trophy hunters and people moving into elephants' habitats. Because elephants are so big, they eat a lot of food—as much as 300 pounds a day, as you've read in this book. A wild elephant will travel 3,000 to 6,000 miles a year in search of food and water. As they travel, they sometimes have conflicts with farmers whose land they try to cross or whose crops they eat.

Elephant herds are matriarchal—led by a female, usually the oldest—and when a matriarch, as the leader is called, is killed, her knowledge of the local terrain is lost to the whole herd. Old and wise matriarchs are the keepers of maps of the region and remember where the grass is plentiful at what times of year, where water can be found even in dry times, and where conflicts with humans have occurred, and they pass that knowledge down to the rest of the herd through the many trips they lead. Knowing where to find food and water can be the difference between life and death for a herd. So elephants need the social structure of the herd and the bonds among its members to keep them safe, and to reproduce successfully. The reproductive cycle of an elephant is long—gestation is nearly 2 years, at about 22 months—and then the baby elephant will nurse for at least 2 years. It will be 4 to 5 years before the mother has another baby. That makes it hard for the species to bounce back from the devastating population losses caused by poaching and habitat loss.

TROPICAL FORESTS

African forest elephants live in tropical forests in west-central Africa. Worldwide, the tropical forests are some of the largest, including the Congo Basin rain forest in Africa and the Amazon in South America. All the tropical forests combined produce 20 percent of our oxygen. You could say that tropical forests are the lungs of our planet! However, due to deforestation, only 5 percent of the world is now covered by tropical forests, down from 12 percent. Restoring about half of those lost acres could lock away as much as 60 gigatons of carbon dioxide by 2050.

Keeping the world's tropical forests large and healthy is one of the best ways to combat climate change. And African forest elephants are a key reason why tropical forests in Africa thrive!

HOW YOU CAN HELP SAVE ELEPHANTS

- Spread the word! Tell your friends that elephants are in trouble.
- Say no to goods made with either new or antique ivory and to other elephant products, such as elephant leather.
- Support elephant-friendly laws. Tell your government representatives that you want tougher regulations and enforcement on trophy hunting and the ivory trade.
- Pay attention to elephants in captivity. For hundreds of years, elephants have been exploited for human entertainment, like the elephant rides and circus shows that still happen around the world today. Even though many zoos are making their elephant habitats

more elephant-friendly, not all of them have. Being aware of these things allows you to make informed decisions about the zoos and entertainment events you go to.

- Choose fair-trade and Rainforest Alliance Certified products and Forest Stewardship Council (FSC)–approved goods; individuals and organizations like these are working to preserve elephant habitats and reduce conflict between humans and elephants.
- Donate to organizations that are helping to save elephants in the wild and support the wildlife rangers who risk their own lives to guard elephants, and to organizations that support sanctuaries for domesticated elephants.
- Choose ecotourism operators who aid conservation efforts when traveling in countries where elephants live in the wild.
- Adopt an elephant online (with your parent's approval).
- Draw, dance, write, speak, and bake! Use your skills to help elephants in need.

AUTHOR'S NOTE

The information in this book is a simplified description of a complex process.
To learn more, start with the Bibliography and additional sources listed on the opposite page.

When I started my research for *If Elephants Disappeared*, I didn't even know there were two different species of African elephants (the African forest elephant and the African savanna elephant). African forest elephants were once believed to be a subspecies of the African savanna elephant, but now scientists have determined that they are two distinct species. I decided to focus this book on the African forest elephant because there was more information about their impact in forests. (That is what I love about information—you never know where it will take you!) The information in this book is based on the best research available and on guidance from scientists. While we don't know exactly what would happen if elephants disappeared, we can draw educated guesses using information that is readily available today.

When I started the If . . . Disappeared books with *If Sharks Disappeared*, it was because I wanted to answer that question for myself: "What would happen if sharks disappeared?" After years of research and lots of art, it became a book that was then followed by another (*If Polar Bears Disappeared*), and now by this book. The If . . . Disappeared books are driven to creation by pure curiosity—how cool is that? I think it is pretty cool. If you are reading this book, you already know that your curiosity can take you to some really amazing places. Maybe it will help you want to save elephants, or to speak out for our planet in other ways. Whatever happens, make sure to let your curiosity roam! Get exploring, get creative, and let's save the planet together!

ACKNOWLEDGMENTS

This book would not have been possible without the following people who assisted me in my research and encouraged my exploration: my family—no words can capture how thankful I am for you all; Minju Chang of BookStop Literary Agency, who couldn't be a bigger rock star if she tried; Emily Feinberg of Roaring Brook Press, who took a chance and continues believing; Monique Sterling, who made a real book out of words and pictures; Simon Hedges, Dr. Fiona Maisels, and Susan Eberth, whose scientific know-how and advice can be seen throughout this book; Jess Keating and Katherine Roy, whose generosity helped me move forward; and you, for reading, learning, and sharing. Let's save some elephants!

BIBLIOGRAPHY

Bouché, Philippe, et al. "Will Elephants Soon Disappear from West African Savannahs?" *PLoS One*, 6, no. 6 (2011): e20619. doi.org/10.1371/journal.pone.0020619.

Campos-Arceiz, Ahimsa, and Steve Blake. "Megagardeners of the Forest—The Role of Elephants in Seed Dispersal." *Acta Oecologica*, 37, no. 6 (2011): 542–553. sciencedirect.com/science/article/pii/S1146609X11000154.

De Knegt, Henrik J., et al. "The Spatial Scaling of Habitat Selection by African Elephants." *Journal of Animal Ecology*, 80, no. 1: 270–281 (2011). savetheelephants.org/wp-content/uploads/2016/11/2010Spatialscaling.pdf.

Downer, John, director. *Elephants: Spy in the Herd.* John Downer Productions Ltd., 2003.

Hedges, Simon, and Fiona Maisels. Personal communication, 2017.

O'Connell, Caitlin, and Donna M. Jackson. *The Elephant Scientist.* New York: Houghton Mifflin Harcourt, 2011.

Parker, Daniel Matthew. "The Effects of Elephants at Low Densities and After Short Occupation Time on the Ecosystems of the Eastern Cape Province, South Africa." PhD thesis, Rhodes University, March 2008.

Platt, John R. "What Happens When Forest Elephants Are Wiped Out in an Ecosystem?" *Scientific American*, March 1, 2013. blogs.scientificamerican.com /extinction-countdown/forest-elephants-wiped-out-ecosystem.

Roy, Katherine. *How to Be an Elephant.* New York: Roaring Brook Press, 2017.

Schwabacher, Martin, with Lori Mortensen. *Elephants.* Salt Lake City: Benchmark Books, 2009.

Stokstad, Erik. "'This Is Amazing!' African Elephants May Transport Seeds Farther Than Any Other Land Animal." *Science*, April 10, 2017. sciencemag.org /news/2017/04/amazing-african-elephants-may-transport-seeds-farther-any-other-land-animal.

ADDITIONAL SOURCES

Wildlife Conservation Society: wcs.org

Save the Elephants: savetheelephants.org

Elephant Voices: elephantvoices.org